Alan G. Rauchway, Ph.D.

Relating

More Reflections of a Psychologist

Second Edition

Custom Publishing

New York   Boston   San Francisco
London   Toronto   Sydney   Tokyo   Singapore   Madrid
Mexico City   Munich   Paris   Cape Town   Hong Kong   Montreal

Cover Art: Photograph by Tim Pannell, courtesy of Corbis Images.

Copyright © 2009, 2007 by Pearson Custom Publishing
All rights reserved.

Permission in writing must be obtained from the publisher before any part of this work may be reproduced or transmitted in any form or by any means, electronic or mechanical, including photocopying and recording, or by any information storage or retrieval system.

All trademarks, service marks, registered trademarks, and registered service marks are the property of their respective owners and are used herein for identification purposes only.

Printed in the United States of America

10 9 8 7 6 5 4 3

2009500007

AM/KL

**Pearson
Custom Publishing**
is a division of

PEARSON

www.pearsonhighered.com

ISBN 10: 0-558-20654-9
ISBN 13: 978-0-558-20654-3

Dedicated
to
my wife
Dale
and my children
Drew Barry
and
Marisa Ann

ACKNOWLEDGMENTS

I would like to thank my wife, Dale, for her invaluable assistance in the preparation and the editing of this manuscript.

I would also like to thank Delia Uherec, and Kim Yuster for their support and encouragement throughout this project. I would also like to thank Dr. Vivian Shapiro, whose caring, wisdom and guidance served as a catalyst for this work.

PREFACE

As a college psychology professor for the past 34 years, I have had the pleasure of teaching over 12,000 students. When questioned, the vast majority stated that they were most interested in learning more about themselves and other people. They also stated that they were particularly intrigued by what makes people "tick" and how to get along with them better.

This book presents more than 250 ideas concerning human relationships. Relating to oneself, dating, marital, parent-child relationships, and therapist-client (patient) relationships are discussed in a clear and concise manner.

The concepts are presented in a unique style to serve as a catalyst to stimulate, challenge, and educate the reader. Each individual will have a very personalized experience as they bring their own life histories into what they are reading.

This book is designed to supplement the academic psychology being presented in the lectures and in the textbooks of the various psychology classes. The style is ideal for classroom discussion. Of course, students will disagree with some of the concepts being presented, and this is valuable as long as they are being stimulated to think about the various ideas being presented.

In essence, the goal of this book is to provide each student an enriched college psychology experience. In addition, it will hopefully provide the student with a better understanding of as well as more effective skills when it comes to relating to themselves and to other people.

Alan G. Rauchway

A healthy dose of *curiosity* is a wonderful antidote for advancing old age. It keeps one alive, fresh and vibrant in dealing with life. As such, I have met some "eternally young" 60, 70, and 80 year olds who benefited from possessing this wonderful quality. I have also encountered some "very old" 20, 30, and 40 year old olds who appeared to lack this essential "anti-aging" attribute.

<> <> <>

Psychologically mature individuals tend to be very careful when it comes to picking their friends. Unlike relatives who we are born to, our friends are selected by ourselves. Knowing this, psychologically mature people try to pick as their friends individuals who will enrich and enhance their lives through their friendship. Such individuals make this world a better place for those who know them to live in. It is a great gift to have a really good friend. Cherish them and the relationship that you have with these individuals.

<> <> <>

If you discover that an individual who you are relating to periodically lies, then you should seriously consider ending the relationship as soon as possible. You will never be able to trust such a person, and without trust, there is *no* real relationship.

It is amazing how many people truly believe that they are *always* correct in their perceptions, thought patterns, and behavior. These individuals put their *egos above all else*. They are far too toxic, self-involved and selfish to have a caring relationship with another person. Do you have someone in your life like this?

<> <> <>

It is interesting how many people who have been victims of psychological abuse (i.e.—verbal abuse, neglect) are so quick to be offended by the slightest perceived slights by individuals who have done nothing more than to try to be caring, respectful and sensitive to these individuals and their needs. These individuals have apparently been so hurt by their abusers that they are putting almost all their energy into looking for potential emotional and/or physical abuse at the hands of others. These people need to emotionally heal somewhat before they are able to accurately perceive the other people in their environment.

<> <> <>

Did you ever hear someone express themselves in a very clever or delightful manner, and you subsequently incorporated these appealing expressions into your own behavior? Do you remember the satisfaction that you experienced by doing this?

There are some individuals who have spend many years in psychoanalytic psychotherapy, and are forever talking about their childhoods, especially with respect to how their parents have damaged them, seemingly forever. In my opinion, these individuals have not completed a successful psychotherapy experience. Why is this? This is because *all* individuals, no matter how trying their childhoods were, and how damaging their parents were towards them, need to eventually move on; live their lives in the present, and look forward in a positive manner toward the future. It is sad how so many adults, including even middle aged and older people, are forever blaming the woes of their lives on their upbringing, and never taking any responsibility for their *own* contributions to the quality of their present lives. These individuals will never be psychologically mature adults.

<> <> <>

Psychologically mature adults do within reason, whatever they can to have a very happy, meaningful and successful life. While not ignoring their past experiences, they take *full* responsibility for the way they are conducting themselves and living their lives. They are not here to blame others. Instead, they try to enjoy other people in their lives as best as they can and to appreciate all the good things that they have in their present lives.

<> <> <>

We all have inside of us, the desire to develop some skill or ability (i.e.—to learn to be a really good swimmer). Why not pick one area and begin working on it as soon as possible. You might be surprised how happy and satisfied you are with yourself by engaging in such a project.

While it is important how a married couple treats each other, it is also significant how each individual treats their in-laws compared to the way they treat their own parents. Sometimes an individual will treat their own family members with more care and respect than they do their spouses' family. If this becomes a pattern during the marriage, then the other person will not have the same love and respect for their mate. On the other hand, people who try to be loving and respectful toward their in-laws comparable to the way they treat their own parents will help strengthen the loving feelings their spouse harbors toward them. Of course, I am not referring to families where one side of the family is very unloving or even mean toward a son or daughter-in-law.

<> <> <>

There are times when one or both members of a marriage have been so busy with the demands of their lives, that they have had very little time to spend together. A sweet note or a sensitive card may be a nice "emotional boost" during this trying period. Just as a plant needs sunshine, water and nutrients to prosper, so does a marriage require "emotional sunshine" and "feeding."

<> <> <>

Some individuals have relatives or friends who can be periodically callous, and even mean in relating to others. Try seeing these people significantly less frequently if all attempts to reason with them have failed. In a number of instances, this technique has helped considerably.

There appears to be an increasing number of individuals who have been taught the rules of society, yet, nonetheless proceed to break them with little or no guilt. I have seen this behavior in my classroom, where the consequences of missing or being late to a significant number of classes is clearly explained. It is amazing to me how many students will still miss a considerable number of classes or periodically come late to them, and when confronted with their behavior and the resulting negative consequences of such behavior are very upset and even hostile at hearing how their final grades will be adversely influenced as a result. It is sad how disrespectful so many individuals have become in our society. They apparently have not been properly socialized by their parents as well as by our society in general. (Of course, I am not referring to individuals where serious life circumstances have caused them to miss or be periodically late coming to class.)

<> <> <>

It is an important ability to be able to clearly differentiate when a parent is doing things for their *own* needs, and when they are truly doing something for their *child's* needs. A number of parents do not possess this ability, with negative consequences resulting in the way they emotionally and socially raise their children.

<> <> <>

Which personality traits do you most value in yourself, and in others? Why is this?

There are some individuals who forever are building up hidden animosities toward others. These individuals will eventually tend to "explode" when they have built up a certain number of these animosities. They could have avoided this whole process of building up a series of hurt feelings and hostilities simply by telling the other person that they were offended by their behavior the *first* time that it had occurred. If you are like this, try out this technique. You will feel much better!

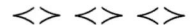

<> <> <>

Did you ever have the experience of reconnecting with an old friend that you have not communicated with for weeks, months or even years? Have you had the experience of feeling that you had not "skipped a beat" when relating to this person once again? I have found this to be a very happy and satisfying experience when it has happened.

<> <> <>

There certainly is a *big* difference between someone giving you something from their heart (i.e.—flowers), as opposed to being given something because you have asked for it. It is the difference between *true* caring and obligation.

It is very important what parents choose to share with their children about the parents' personal life. All kinds of psychological damage has been done to unsuspecting children by their parents telling them personal aspects of their parents' marriage and other facets of this parents' life that their children should *not* be hearing. Remember, your children are your *children,* not your pal or buddy.

<> <> <>

Some individuals are the "great needs filterers." This means that their *own* needs are by far the most important consideration in their lives. Such individuals are very difficult if not impossible to have a decent relationship with since they are forever making certain that their needs are being met in their relationships. For example, if they buy you a present you can be sure that they have picked out something that they have decided that you would like, whether or not this truly is the case. Also, they will tend to consider whether they should get one for *themselves.* Whenever, they do something for you, they are *forever* reminding you how terrific they are for having done this or that for you. Interestingly enough, while these people tend to view themselves as great "givers", they are in reality, the "greater takers." In essence, these are toxic individuals who should be avoided whenever possible.

<> <> <>

It is interesting to note that some of the very individuals who most bemoan how terrible other people are have friends and/or relatives who are *much more giving* to this individual, than the latter is toward them. These people lack the gracious gift of appreciation.

If you are involved in a good relationship, then it should bring out the best qualities in you. Namely, it should bring out the soft, gentle, tender and loving qualities in you. Instead, if you are constantly arguing with your partner, often feel as if you are "walking on egg shells" around them and generally feeling irritable and unhappy, then you seriously need to evaluate whether this is the right relationship for you.

<> <> <>

Some people say "I'm sorry" to others not because they are truly apologetic, but rather to "shut up" the other person in an attempt to end the disagreement. In these cases, it is important for the individual being manipulated to clearly point out what the "apologizer" is really trying to accomplish and how you feel about this behavior.

<> <> <>

It is important for every individual to save a few minutes of each day to nurture and emotionally replenish themselves. Whether it is taking a bubble bath; watching your favorite television show; or having a glass of your favorite beverage, it is important to give yourself some tender, loving care (TLC) on a daily basis.

Sometimes an individual is confused or unsure as to how to handle a given relationship or situation. If you ask them what they would tell a son or daughter facing this same dilemma, these same individuals often instantaneously strongly express what they would advise them to do. I have found this technique as being quite helpful in psychotherapy in clarifying how clients might want to handle many situations that occur in their lives.

<> <> <>

The opposite of love is not hate or apathy. The opposite of love is *selfishness*. Love involves having tender feelings for another person, putting energy into the other person, and then showing it through sensitive, considerate actions. Selfishness involves putting all or almost all of your energy into meeting your *own* needs, little or none being expended toward the other person.

<> <> <>

If you have been in a relationship for an extended period of time, an interesting question that you might ask each other is, "What qualities about me do you like?"

As I grow older, I am increasingly *amazed* by the brilliance of the human mind. Whether I am focusing on man having walked on the moon, neurosurgeons performing delicate brain surgery to end some form of epilepsy or remove a malignant tumor; or talking to another individual on the telephone who is thousands of miles away; I am absolutely in *awe* of what some human beings have invented which have tremendously improved the quality of our lives.

<> <> <>

Parents, first and foremost are *human beings*. They range from wonderful to horrendous, encompassing every category in between. It is sad that there are a number of "bullies" who hide behind their titles as your "mother" or your "father" as if this gives them the right to emotionally and/or physically abuse you. This is *totally unacceptable*. No one, and I mean no one, has the right to disrespect and abuse another human being, even if these abusers are your parents.

<> <> <>

Just because the other person does not openly react when their spouse is talking or acting abusively towards them, does *not* mean that there has been no emotional damage to their relationship. If this becomes a *pattern* over time, the love you initially felt toward your spouse may totally have eroded over this period, and the person may suddenly declare that they no longer love you, and they want "out" of the relationship, stunning their spouse. While the spouse may state that this was a sudden and totally unexpected outcome, *actually* it had been developing over the years.

In a good marriage, ideally both people put their relationship as their number one priority, and they consistently behave in such a manner. However, when one person puts their marriage as their number one priority, and the other puts it second or third or even lower in importance to them, with such activities as work and career being of greater importance to themselves, then there will be problems and tensions that will arise in the marriage.

<> <> <>

Some people say things out loud not so much for their partner to hear, but really to reassure and calm *themselves*. For example, some individuals get insulted when their spouse asks them three or four times during the same day if they remember to mail an important letter the next day. In these cases, the questioning individual is simply trying to reassure and calm themselves down and is *not* trying to belittle or insult their partner. If you are aware of doing this on occasion, it is helpful to explain this to your spouse for better mutual understanding.

<> <> <>

Some immature and insecure individuals are forever judging the words and actions of their mate in a critical manner. These individuals are being controlling and hurtful. Psychologically mature individuals, on the other hand, tend to let their spouse be *themselves*. These individuals try to be accepting, supportive and valuing of their spouse, including their actions and words.

In a good relationship, there is *always* mutual respect. For example, people try to keep their word; they do not call each other abusive names (i.e., moron), they are good listeners, etc. If this respect is missing on the part of one or both parties, then there can be *no* love.

<> <> <>

Having worked with many couples in psychotherapy over the years, it is obvious that in the vast majority of instances, the problems of the couple revolves around lack of respect issues on the part of one or both of the individuals.

<> <> <>

In essence, *mutual respect* is the foundation upon which *any* good relationship is based.

<> <> <>

I have heard a number of individuals complain that their partner gets so "emotional" when they are angry or hurt. Yet, these same individuals love when their mate is so passionate and romantic. These individuals do not understand that a person cannot be "half a loaf" emotionally. This means that a person is either going to be highly emotional, openly and passionately expressing *all* their feelings or they will tend to be inhibited in the expression of their feelings. In essence, you either tend to be an emotionally expressive individual or you are not.

Intrapersonal and interpersonal perceptiveness and sensitivity are great human attributes. Intrapersonal and interpersonal perceptiveness deals with our ability to notice events occurring inside and outside of our body. Intrapersonal and interpersonal sensitivity involves our ability to understand what these events actually *mean*. Developing these attributes through psychotherapy can help people be happier and more successful in their relationships.

<> <> <>

Some people tend to personalize their partner's behavior. Namely, *anything* and *everything* their mate does or says is a reflection of *you*. These people tend to be immature and extremely self-centered. Your mate had years of living *before* they met you, and they have a *whole* life, with other people in it besides you, that they relate to and who influence their feelings and behavior. This is important to keep in mind when relating to another person.

<> <> <>

Some individuals get great pleasure in trying to make another person that they care about happy. In contrast, there are other people who get absolutely *no* enjoyment in doing this. The latter only are interested in what others are giving to *them*.

There are many, many individuals who have been the victims of child abuse who do *not* know it. These individuals only equate child abuse with physical violence. They do not understand that there is also such a thing as psychological or emotional abuse, including verbal abuse where parents or other family members periodically call their children abusive names when they are angry or frustrated (i.e., imbecile, stupid).

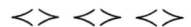

<> <> <>

In some families, one or both parents psychologically and/or physically abuse one or more of their children. In addition, some of the other family members (i.e., a brother, a sister) will justify the parent's abusive behavior toward one or more of the other children as being appropriate and warranted. These "enablers" make the abusive situation even more painful for the victim or victims as they overtly or implicitly are stating that it is the *victim's fault* that they are being abused.

<> <> <>

It is astonishing how many people continue to "hit their heads against the proverbial wall" time after time. These individuals need to periodically assess whether a given course of action is working in their relationships, or even in life, in general. If not, they need to be *flexible*, and try another approach.

There are some relationships where one individual is constantly making demands on the other person to do things for them. Whether it involves paying bills, running errands or cooking meals, the list is apparently endless. At the same time, this individual is constantly "battering" and belittling the giving person as just being "utterly terrible" with the demanding individual always "putting up" with the "giver." The giving person is so preoccupied with meeting the demands of their partner and defending themselves against the endless criticisms being levied against them, that they never appear to look *clearly* at the other person. If they did, they would see that they are dealing with a selfish, lazy, ungiving and very hostile individual. They might also learn through psychotherapy that they put up with this abusive behavior because of a poor self-image (how they feel about themselves), and a lack of self-confidence and self-respect.

<> <> <>

Some couples come for couples therapy, and it becomes readily apparent to their psychologist after several sessions that the major reason their relationship is not going well is because one or both of the individuals have significant psychological problems that prevent them from being happy and from enjoying relating to their partner. They also tend not to possess adequate relating skills that are needed in order to have a satisfying relationship with another person. It is imperative that this individual or both individuals enter individual psychotherapy as well as go for couple's therapy in order for this relationship to ever work out successfully.

Some individuals love to put others on a "pedestal." These same individuals tend to lack self-confidence, have poor self-images, and are overly dependent on others to make their major life decisions for them. While the other individual may initially be flattered by the attention and praise they are receiving from the dependent person, they will eventually tend to find the latter becoming a burden as well as emotionally draining.

<> <> <>

Did you ever notice that when you are trying to get things "in order" in your environment, you also may feel better emotionally? This is because when trying to straighten out (i.e. organize a messy pile of papers) or clean up something (i.e. wash and wax the kitchen floor), we are actually symbolically trying to gain control over our inner psychological world of feelings, fantasies and/or thoughts. This feeling of gaining psychological control is a very satisfying one.

<> <> <>

Some parents truly believe that their children are miniature copies of themselves. As such, they also believe that their children should feel, think and behave exactly as they would in various situations. These children will find it extremely difficult to become independent, confident adults with their own strong sense of identity. They may well require some psychotherapy to help them discover who they really are and to help them become emotionally separated from their domineering parents.

I have met adults in their 30's, 40's, 50's and even older who still refer to their mother as "mommy" and their father as "daddy." This suggests that even though they may feel and act like adults in their other relationships, they still feel like children when relating to their parents. Beginning to call your parents "mother" or "mom," and "father" or "dad" is the first step toward finally feeling and acting like an independent adult in relating to one's parents.

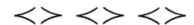

<> <> <>

It seems to be the adolescent's rallying cry to declare that "I am very capable of running my own life!" in dealing with their parents and other authority figures. Unfortunately, this is *not* true. Adolescent enthusiasm and rebelliousness fueled by raging hormones within does *not* equal wisdom.

<> <> <>

It is a wonderful experience in psychotherapy for a parent to truly understand how they are unintentionally hurting their child, and to learn a more constructive way of dealing with them. To see the smile and relief on that parent's face when the new approach works is indeed very gratifying for both the parent and the psychologist.

Some clients come to psychotherapy looking for absolute answers. "Should I drop my boyfriend or continue the relationship?" is a common example. A competent psychologist will help the client look at the pros and cons of continuing this relationship with the client ultimately making the final decision (unless this client is very disturbed).

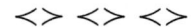

<> <> <>

While some parents and some other cultures believe otherwise I firmly believe that every person has the right to pick their own *career* (within reason), and to select a *marriage partner*. Love should be the basis for picking a spouse, not parental arrangements. In essence, parents do *not* own their children like they do property.

<> <> <>

Some parents spend considerable time and money in exposing their children to "lessons in life" involving playing a musical instrument and becoming an excellent athlete. How about "life lessons" in becoming a happy, productive person?

<> <> <>

What nickname would you select for yourself? Why this nickname?

What is your favorite time of the day? Why is this so?

<> <> <>

Couples have to decide whether one or more of their differences are major or minor. If there is at least one major difference between the two of them (i.e., whether or not to have children), then they should either consider the possibility of going to counseling or psychotherapy, or seriously consider ending the relationship as this major difference or differences can cause significant chronic conflict and unhappiness for one or both individuals.

<> <> <>

Some individuals complain that their mate is "so emotional." Actually, it is better, within reason, to know how your partner is feeling toward you, than to have hidden hurts and animosities build up to where this individual suddenly states that they no longer care about you and they want to break up.

<> <> <>

Just as the psychiatrist's specialty is their knowledge of the psychiatric drugs, so should the clinical psychologist's expertise be in the realm of interpersonal relationships.

It is a sad commentary that so many divorced people do not go for psychotherapy. Instead of trying to understand what caused their relationship to end in order to mature and grow so as to better pick and relate to a new partner, they instead tend to view themselves as "victims" who were terribly taken advantage of by their former spouse. Friends and relatives often tend to do the "easy" thing by supporting their perceptions. As such, the individuals are *no* better equipped to have successful intimate relationships then they were when they were married.

<> <> <>

Beware of the many "victims" walking around in our society. I have met many of them professionally and personally. They will proclaim that they have been previously abused and they are determined that no one will "get over on me" again. As a result, these individuals believe that they are *entitled* to do almost anything in order to protect and take care of themselves and get their needs met. Unfortunately, many an unsuspecting new person in these people's lives will tend to have to "pay the price" for these previous alleged abuses.

<> <> <>

Even though life experiences, particularly our upbringing, can influence to some extent how much pleasure we get in trying to help make another person happy (i.e., giving another person a special gift), I am becoming increasingly convinced that this attribute is primarily genetically determined.

When a loving couple faces a serious illness in one or both of them, their love tends to deepen and become more precious as they become increasingly aware of the finiteness of their relationship.

<> <> <>

How would you feel and react if one of your parents genuinely said, "It is a pleasure and honor to have you in my life"?

<> <> <>

What nickname would you select for each key person in your life (i.e., family members, friends)? Why did you pick these nicknames for each of them?

<> <> <>

Another interesting question that you might ask if you are involved in an extended relationship is, "If you could change one thing about me what would it be, and why would you change this particular behavior?"

<> <> <>

Some individuals view psychotherapy as some sort of entertainment. They may come regularly on a weekly basis, but they do not leave the office and try to *apply* the insights or "lessons in life" that they have learned in the sessions. This is unfortunate.

Some individuals come to psychotherapy in order to get a "quick fix" for their problems. They may come typically from one to even a few sessions, and then they unilaterally decide that they are ready to leave. They invariably return when the next "fire" occurs in their lives. These clients almost never achieve any real emotional or social growth, as they are not willing to make a true commitment to working out their problems in psychotherapy. These clients cannot accept that they need to trust and cooperate with their psychologist. They also cannot accept that this process takes *time* as well as *hard work*.

<> <> <>

Some people believe that if you give your word about something you can *never* change your mind. This is being very rigid and unreasonable in certain instances. It is a good reason why you should not promise sex to your partner later in the day. You could change your mind by then!

<> <> <>

Some of the great accomplishments in our society have been achieved by individuals who are quite insecure with low self-images. These individuals are rarely satisfied with anything they do, so they are always trying to improve upon their creations. For example, at our local gym, the proprietor who is very talented is forever adding improvements to the facility, doing nearly all of the work by himself. When praised for his wonderful work, he invariably comments, "It could be better." Psychologically, his outside improvements are, in part, his attempt to improve on how he feels "inside."

Some people in our society have all kinds of problems getting along with other people because they do not consider the *consequences* of their actions. For example, one individual may treat another poorly, and then be shocked when the latter does not help them out in a future situation. These individuals do not tie together these two events. If this is not remedied, then this person will have many difficult interpersonal moments in their lifetime.

<> <> <>

Many parents tell their children that they raised all of them exactly the same way. In reality, this is *impossible* just based on the child's position in the family. For example, the first born child comes into the family without any competition since there are no brothers or sisters already present. On the other hand, the third born child enters the world with two older siblings already present. Due to these two different situations, no two children within the same family can ever be raised in the *exact* same manner.

<> <> <>

Some adults have been trying to make their parent or parents happy for their entire lives. Their attempts often cause stress for themselves and even within their marriages. Unfortunately, in some cases, this will *never* happen and these individuals need to *accept* this, and to direct some of this wasted energy into their marriages, their children and into themselves with hopefully better results.

Just as some people are born with different levels of artistic ability, so are they endowed with different capacities to be loving human beings. Environment can help people reach their maximum potential in this area, but nonetheless, there will be widespread differences in their ability to love others due to genetic factors.

<> <> <>

Just as we have a quantity of physical energy to draw upon on a daily basis, we also have a quantity of emotional energy at our disposal. People can do things to increase their emotional energy levels (i.e., doing an activity that they enjoy) as well as do things to decrease levels (i.e., spending time with a self-centered, selfish individual).

<> <> <>

Many people state that they are looking to find a "loving person." A good question to ask them is, "Are *you* a loving person?"

<> <> <>

Many people talk about finding the "right person." A good question to ask them is, "Would you like to date someone like *you*? Why or why not?"

Every individual will experience "bumps" in the road as they continue on their journey through life. It is their *attitude* toward these "bumps," and their resulting *coping strategies* that determine to a large extent how psychologically healthy or unhealthy a given individual is.

<> <> <>

In a number of instances, I have seen the *more selfish* member of a relationship go outside the relationship and relate intimately with another person. Also, these same selfish individuals sometimes are the ones who initiate a divorce; in both cases claiming their needs have not been adequately met by their mate. This is ironic, since, if anyone is going to have an affair or dissolve the marriage it would logically be the individual who has been the "giver" in this relationship, and certainly not the perpetual "taker!"

<> <> <>

In this age of narcissism (selfishness), it is fascinating that some individuals have a "tipping jar" near the store cash register or near the counter where they are dispensing bagels or cold cuts. Are we to tip them for simply doing their jobs? I do not think that this is warranted.

Some people who express anger over certain behaviors exhibited by others, actually exhibit the *very same* behaviors themselves. They refuse to acknowledge this to themselves and to others. If they were able to do this, they would become more tolerant of other people.

<> <> <>

Ideally, when an individual is going to leave psychotherapy, they should discuss this with their psychologist, etc. Individuals who abruptly terminate the sessions without any prior discussion are demonstrating a self-centered and selfish orientation that they probably exhibit in their outside relationships.

<> <> <>

Visiting a *new* place, joining a *new* club, beginning a *new* relationship or starting a *new* hobby can provide an "emotional boost" to your life. You may well feel energized and your enthusiasm level elevated. Try it!

Some parents in their zeal to socialize their children may actually *squash* their child's true or *genuine self*. These children may grow up being high achievers, being successful in school and in their careers, and appear to get along well with other people. On the surface they appear to "have it all." In spite of these successes, they chronically feel unhappy and depressed with little or no insight as to why this is happening. This is because they are *not* living a *genuine* life. They do not know who they are, and in essence, are not happy with *themselves*. They have not been allowed by their parents to find out what their *true* likes and dislikes are, what true talents they possess and what is truly important to *them* in leading their own lives. A good psychotherapy experience would be very helpful to them in discovering their *true* selves. This will enable them to grab a hold of their lives and live it to the fullest in the context of our society.

<> <> <>

Husbands often proudly speak about how they *help* their wives out with their household chores. However, in this modern era, where a significant number of families have *both* husband and wife working out of the house full time, with the wife sometimes working longer hours than her spouse, it is *insensitive* for the husband to announce how wonderful he is to be helping his wife out with *her* housework as well as helping to take care of their children. This declaration implies that it is his wife's inalienable *duty* to do the house chores and to take care of the children, and he is simply a "wonderful guy" to help her out. This is actually being extremely callous and sexist!

A dear couple that I am friendly with were discussing how to get from one part of town to another. The husband stated that the "right way" to go was the route that took the least amount of time, and used up the minimum amount of gas. On the other hand, his wife commented that she always took the longer route because she found it the most "enjoyable." She stated that this was the "right way" for her. It is the ability to tolerate and respect these differences, as well as the ability to talk these things out that will help contribute to a happy and healthy relationship.

<> <> <>

An increasing number of middle-aged and senior women are becoming disenchanted with computer dating. They complain that the vast majority of men while professing a desire for a "serious relationship" are actually looking for "cheap" dates leading to easy sex. In some cases, these men claim the exchange of e-mails is, in essence, the "courtship" and no "formal" dates involving spending any of their money is necessary. They are now ready for a sexual encounter. This suggests that a significant number of these middle-aged and senior men have not matured emotionally or socially since their adolescent years, and may even have regressed.

Some married women decide they would like to get a job once their children are in part-time or full-time school . In some of these cases, they proceed to announce that any money that they earn is their own, while the money that their husband's earn is "family money," that is used to support the family. This is a callous, selfish position which may well damage the marital relationship. On the other hand, women who state that the money they earn is also "family money," used to make life easier for all members of the family, and will be pooled with her spouse's income will be doing a loving, caring act which should bring the couple emotionally closer.

<> <> <>

In some troubled marriages, one or both parents treat one of their children as their new husband or wife on an emotional level. They talk to this child about their marital problems, and act in a jealous manner when this child relates to their peers, and particularly when they start to date. This parental behavior can be extremely damaging to their child's psychological development. For example, when the child tries to relate independently to others, they may feel considerable guilt, and feel like "traitors" toward their parasitic parent. This can seriously detract from them fully enjoying their lives, especially in trying to have happy, intimate relationships with a spouse.

Close your eyes and visualize one member of your family. Now write five words that best describes this person. Follow this procedure for each family member. Now look at each of your lists. This may well prove to be insightful and informative.

<> <> <>

Psychologically mature individuals, even when they are faced with the most traumatic situations, always try to learn from these occurrences. At the very least, they would like to learn how to prevent such an event from happening again.

<> <> <>

Psychologically mature individuals grow to increasingly appreciate and value their lives as they pass from middle to old age. This is because they become increasingly aware of the passage of time, and with this progression they try to fully experience and enjoy every moment that they have left to live.

<> <> <>

When it has been a particularly stressful and even a traumatic day, it is almost akin to having an effective psychotherapy session knowing that a brand new and fresh day begins tomorrow, bringing with it an array of hopes and possibilities. I have found this to have been of great value many times during my life.

Try never to worry endlessly about the hypothetical. In my personal experience, 95% of the time these potential obstacles do not even occur in one's own life resulting in a waste of energy, as well as causing needless anxiety and unhappiness. In the rare instances that they do actually occur, you will deal with each of them as best as you can.

<> <> <>

Isn't it sad that some people get so excited over an individual in a service position (i.e., department store employee) simply doing their job competently? Actually, receiving competent and caring assistance in these instances should be the *right* of each and every customer.

<> <> <>

One important "lesson in life" that I learned in my personal psychotherapy occurred when I was explaining to my psychologist that I never tried to put people out when they offered to help me. I really thought that this was considerate behavior on my part. When the psychologist explained to me that I was behaving in a self-centered and selfish manner I was absolutely amazed. In essence, I was not considering at all how the other person involved was feeling about my refusal to let them help me. In actuality, she noted that some people might actually *enjoy* helping me out, and I was not giving them the opportunity to do so. This "lesson in life" has helped me on many occasions in future similar situations.

Some people have unfortunately been raised by self-centered and selfish parents. As a result, the individual family members tend to develop an "every man for himself" philosophy. For example, when the family is eating dinner at the kitchen table as a group, sharing is not of primary importance to the family members. Instead, each family member appears to be particularly concerned about making sure that they get a goodly portion of the food on the table. Whether or not each family member gets their fair share is of little or no importance to each of these individuals. The resulting selfish, self-centered, ungiving attitudes and behavior of these individuals will tend to cause other individuals in their lives, such as friends and especially lovers, considerable distress and unhappiness.

<> <> <>

When couples plan a trip they need to make sure that both individuals are going to have a true "vacation." Some husbands plan to rent cottages, houses and even villas, where their wives will continue to cook the family meals, and in some cases, have to clean these rented facilities. Also, the husband may have set up a whole itinerary where he is constantly playing golf or going fishing with other husbands, leaving the wife to take care of their children. This type of vacation will *not* be emotionally nor physically replenishing for these women, and they will tend to resent their mate's selfishness and self-centeredness.

Sometimes individuals can best express their feelings and thoughts towards the other person by writing them a letter. In some cases, they may ultimately decide to mail it, while in others, they choose not to do so. By writing this letter, they can more precisely capture how they are feeling inside, and be able to accurately communicate their thoughts and feelings. This can ultimately result in a better understanding of, and communication of each person's position in an emotionally charged situation.

<> <> <>

Once both people in a relationship, emotionally as well as intellectually, understand the importance of "reaching out" in order to understand their partner's major physical and emotional needs in an endeavor to meet them within reason, then they are on the road to having a happier, more satisfying relationship.

<> <> <>

The way the client interacts with the psychologist provides valuable information as to how the client relates to *other* people outside the therapy office. Also, the feelings that the psychologist experiences in relating to the client provides insight as to how other people feel toward this individual. This information can be very helpful in teaching the client to relate to others in a more constructive and caring manner.

Some people are so controlling in their relationships that they even try to control the psychotherapy sessions with their psychologist. They need to stop doing this, and to develop some trust and confidence in letting their psychologist, within reason, do what needs to be done in order to help them.

<> <> <>

Clients *do* have a right to question a technique they believe their psychologist is using or to ask the therapist to explain a statement that the latter has made during a session. This is *not* being controlling, rather, this is part of the therapeutic relationship.

<> <> <>

Students can learn a great deal about their professor's personalities as well as the level of their relating skills over the course of a semester. The best teachers will treat each student and the class collectively with caring and respect, and expecting the same treatment in return. Whether the student receives a final grade of "A" or "F," the experience of being in such a professor's class should be emotionally, socially and intellectually enriching for each of them. In essence, this professor should be a *stellar* role model for each of their students. Thus, the student should have *grown* as human beings from being in this professor's class. It is a sad commentary that so few teachers understand that this is their role, and ultimately their mission as teachers.

Some parents tell their children that they had better do well in school or they will grow up to be "failures." What a callous and inaccurate statement! I have met many people who were not good students, and some who did not graduate or even attend college, and who moved on to meaningful and successful careers. They also appeared to be quite happy with their lives. There are, in essence, *many* ways to live our lives in a meaningful and satisfying manner. For our parents to state that there is only *one* true path to happiness and success is untrue, and it puts an unfair burden on children who just are not going to be "good" students (i.e., some learning disabled individuals).

<> <> <>

Some individuals are afraid to be alone. In some cases, this is because they are afraid of being alone with *themselves*. Namely, they are afraid of their own feelings, fantasies and/or thoughts. In essence they are fearful of dealing with their own psychological world. As a result, when they are alone, these same individuals may resort to addictive behaviors such as drinking, drugging, smoking, overeating or providing as much environmental stimulation as possible (i.e., blasting the radio or their CD players) to block out or mask what is inside of them psychologically. These people waste large quantities of energy in these endeavors. They would benefit from a good psychotherapy experience.

Many parents consider themselves to be excellent caretakers partly because of all the activities they have their children enrolled in. In many cases, they do *not* want to see that they are being very *neglectful* of what their children need *most*, namely learning the essential "lessons of life" in dealing with themselves and others in becoming happy, productive human beings. Their children need to see good role models in the way their parents deal with life and the people in it. This takes considerable time and energy in interacting lovingly and constructively with their children.

<> <> <>

Some individuals, when they express one of their needs, are sometimes told that they are "very selfish." It is interesting to note that people who are constantly telling you how selfish you are when you ask them to meet one of your needs are often very selfish, demanding and overbearing *themselves*. These individuals tend to take advantage of others who tend to believe that they have no right to have any of their needs met by another person, and if one of their needs are met, they tend to feel guilt-ridden. Beware of these domineering, parasitic individuals who use guilt to take advantage of others.

<> <> <>

Some individuals tend to blame "luck" for their unhappy existences. In contrast, psychologically mature people, while acknowledging that luck or outside, uncontrollable events can significantly influence their lives, also state that, in general, they take as much responsibility as they can for the way they live their lives.

We could *all* use courses at every level of our schooling on what constitutes a good, loving mother, father, sister, brother, grandmother, etc. Many individuals really have little or no idea as to how they should act in any or all of these roles. This would help prevent a lot of confusion and abuse.

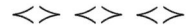

<> <> <>

Some individuals are forever putting energy into looking for *flaws* in other people. Whether it is criticizing one's physical appearance, one's personality, or one's intellect, these people appear to "relish" putting down another human being. These people are extremely toxic to be with, and if possible, it is best to avoid them. If this is not possible, then it is important to tell them that they need to stop "trashing" others, including you, in their presence if you are going to continue to relate to them.

<> <> <>

Try smiling at some strangers when you feel comfortable doing so. I have often received the most beautiful smiles in return.

<> <> <>

The way people select pets to be in their home, and the way they treat these pets can be a sensitive barometer of how psychologically well-adjusted these individuals are. In general, the kinder and more respectful an individual is to a dependent, loving, loyal pet, the psychologically healthier this person is.

Some individuals periodically speak in a belittling, sarcastic manner. However, these same individuals are very sensitive if others treat *them* in a similar way. They may even take offense when no one is actually speaking or acting in an offensive manner. These people obviously have a major "double standard" when it comes to how they can act relative to how others can speak or act toward them. It is extremely difficult, if not impossible, to have a relationship with such individuals.

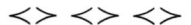

<> <> <>

Some teachers are very critical and demanding of their students. In a number of cases, they are actually recreating their home environments growing up. However, they *reverse* the parent and the child roles. Symbolically, they become their punitive, demanding parent or parents from their own childhood, and the students symbolically become the teacher as a child. This pathological situation is the teacher's unaware attempt to resolve some of his/her psychological issues, but at the *expense* of the academic and psychological well-being of their students. This will significantly interfere with their effectiveness as teachers and role models.

<> <> <>

The more people study how to have effective relationships with others, the more they are impressed with the powerfulness and importance of the *spoken word.*

The better an individual relates to others, in general, the more *precisely* and *accurately* they communicate what they mean to say using the vehicle of language.

<> <> <>

If you are having a relationship with someone from a different culture, it is very important to understand the values and customs of each of your respective cultural backgrounds. I have seen many relationships break up or be seriously damaged because these differences were not sufficiently addressed.

<> <> <>

It would be very useful if there was a course at *every* grade level dealing with how to be happy. If you ask parents what they would like most for their children, the vast majority will state, "I just would like them to be happy." As such, this course would teach children, adolescents and adults how to be happy, and how to have a happy life. The course would include such topics as, "The Art of Appreciation," "How to Genuinely Compliment Another Person," as well as, "The Art of Giving and Receiving." If taught properly by the right type of teacher, it would be a *smashing success*!

When an individual is telling you about a conflict that they are having with another person, and they begin to tell you what each person allegedly said to the other, it is important to remember that nonverbal cues are an important part of this communication. For example, the tone in which these words were uttered, the person's facial expression as well as their body posture can all contribute to the *same* words being received in *very different* ways. This is important to keep in mind when listening to such conversations.

<> <> <>

While some couples profess in psychotherapy how much they love each other, it sometimes becomes quite apparent that one or both individuals exhibit a certain harshness in relating to the other person. They need to become aware of this in order to become more caring.

<> <> <>

Some couples suffer from communication problems partly because one or both of them are poor listeners. They either are so intent on making their *own* points that they really do not listen carefully to what their partner is saying, or they actually hear it, but quickly dismiss it without seriously digesting what their mate is trying to tell them. This suggests a real self-centeredness and selfishness on these individuals' part. As I always tell my students and psychotherapy clients, "The opposite of love is selfishness." In my opinion, it is the number one destroyer of relationships.

<> <> <>

It is important in a loving relationship that each member of the relationship lets the other person grow. For example, a married couple I treated in psychotherapy, started out with the husband being a professional and the sole supporter of the family financially with the wife doing volunteer work. Over the years, the wife started her own agency, becoming the executive director in the process. This necessitated her putting in many more hours at work, and entailed some traveling around the country. The husband was supportive and accommodating of his wife's new career. She has stated on many occasions that, "I love my husband more than ever" as he was able to be a loving partner as his wife grew in her career. This is in stark contrast to numerous marriages which are ruined because one member of the relationship could only look at their *own* needs with no consideration for their mate's needs and desires.

<> <> <>

Psychologically healthy people look at the "Big Picture" when it comes to their relationships. Namely, they always try to keep in mind how the other person has treated them in general over the months, or even years that they have known one another. As a result, they tend to give individuals who have been caring and respectful toward them, a certain amount of leeway or tolerance when these same people may be somewhat irritable or callous on a given day. These people have earned this flexibility and tolerance for their overall kind and caring behaviors that they have exhibited the vast majority of the time. Of course, if these same individuals are hurtful or mean to you, then by all means, set some limits with them, in order to stop these unacceptable behaviors.

A good question that a couple can ask each other is, "In what ways do you show me that you love and respect me?"

<> <> <>

The more that you love someone, the more pleasure you receive when you have done something that really makes them happy.

<> <> <>

Just as there is water or air pollution, there is also what I like to call "verbal pollution" all around us. So many individuals, including many adolescents and even children, are constantly using obscenities in expressing themselves. Words such as morons, idiots and much worse are commonly being verbally thrown about in common every day speech. People who tend to use such obscenities in expressing themselves are demonstrating ignorance and a lack of respect for other people as well as themselves. It would be wonderful if a concerted effort be made to significantly reduce the use of these "ugly" expressions in favor of more respectful choice of words.

<> <> <>

An interesting question to ask oneself is, "Under what circumstances do I especially like myself, and under what circumstances do I not really like myself?"

Many people are forever wanting to experience *passion* in their lives. Many speak of their relationships ending because there was no longer any excitement or passion. Some people seek out this passion by coaching their children's sports' teams or playing on their own teams. This could be viewed in some cases as a "safety valve" to protect their marriages.

<> <> <>

Many people are concerned with how to pick the "right person." One general guideline would be to look for someone who you find attractive (though not necessarily a "knockout"), and see if their inside (their psychological makeup) is even more appealing than their outside self.

<> <> <>

When people with a good self-image (like and value themselves) spend time with a person whom they find physically attractive, if the latter does kind, sensitive things for others, they tend to find these individuals even *more* physically appealing. On the other hand, people with a poor self-image will view such people as either being no more physically attractive in these situations or even *less* physically appealing. They may even begin to find this kind of individual "boring" or "unexciting."

Our parents teach us, to a large extent, what we *deserve* in life. Parents who are loving toward their children and their spouse teach their children that they deserve this kind of treatment in their relationships with others. Similarly, children whose parents tend to be selfish, cold and/or mean towards them and their spouse teach their children that they deserve the same or similar treatment from friends and lovers. This is one of the most important "lessons in life" that we learn from our parents.

<> <> <>

When an individual wants to terminate their marriage, it sometimes is not so much that their spouse was callous or mean toward them, but rather, that they have not been in a position to be independent and in charge of their *own* lives. They may have gone directly from their parent's home, and gotten married, and proceeded to then live with their spouse. It would be very helpful to both members of the marriage to go for psychotherapy to closely examine this state of affairs and try to work this out as best as possible.

<> <> <>

If an individual acts in a manner that is especially pleasing to you, it is important to really praise them effusively. Too many people are quick to vehemently criticize their spouse or children when they behave in a manner contrary to the way they would like, yet these same people say little or even nothing when this same individual behaves in a very positive manner. This is, indeed, a mistake.

Sometimes, even a little encouragement can bring out the greatest effort in another human being. Try it!

<> <> <>

When a person truly feels loved, this feeling radiates towards others in their presence. The warmth, gentleness and kindness exhibited by these people tend to have a healing, ameliorative effect similar to how one feels when they are outside on a beautiful, warm, sunny day.

<> <> <>

When an individual feels loved, this love tends to have a positive influence on the individual's physical and psychological well-being.

<> <> <>

When a person feels unloved, this tends to have a toxic effect on their physical and psychological make-up. This can also be very energy draining as well.

In generai, the best teachers are the most caring toward their students. Also, their students *feel* the most cared about by these same teachers.

<> <> <>

Good *timing* is very important if you want to have a good relationship with another person. You can make the same request of your mate on two separate occasions, and in the first instance you are warmly received and in the second you are indifferently or even angrily responded to. The reason for this disparity is timing. This is the ability to size up your mate's emotional state and the overall circumstances before making a given statement or request. Some people are very skilled at doing this, and others are quite poor at it, leading to all kinds of conflicts with their partner.

<> <> <>

One of the best lessons that I have learned as a psychotherapy client and as a practitioner is that it is a perfectly acceptable answer to another person's question to genuinely state, "I don't know."

Some husbands complain that their wives do not appreciate that they always try to help them whenever they are asked to do so. What these men do not understand is that their wives would like them to anticipate family needs in advance, and then *initiate* taking care of certain family needs *on their own*. Of course, wives who have this complaint about their husbands cannot proceed to criticize them if they do not do something exactly the way their wives would have handled a task. In essence, some of these women give their husbands *double messages*, telling them to think ahead and take the initiative, but if you do, I'll criticize you.

<> <> <>

Some husbands who are having affairs often state that they enjoy spending much more time with their mistresses rather than their wives. This is an *unfair* comparison. To compare a relaxed occasional evening out with a mistress in a dating, romantic type setting with relating to your wife, which involves dealing with family stresses, including issues with the children, financial stresses, and the like is grossly unfair, and says a lot about the insensitivity, self-centered and selfishness of these men. Remember, the *opposite* of love is selfishness.

<> <> <>

A good question to ask your partner is, "What things in this life do you think are important to me?" After your partner answers try to answer this same question for them.

It is interesting that in the most loving relationships, each member of the relationship really tries to get to know the other person, particularly with respect to what is important to them, what they most enjoy out of their lives, and what their hopes and dreams are. They then proceed to try to help meet and facilitate the meeting of their mate's needs as best they can, while also trying to get their own needs met. Both individuals are also each others' number one fans, supporting and encouraging each other whenever they can. In essence, this loving relationship *enriches* each member of the relationship.

<> <> <>

It is amazing how many individuals profess love for one another, yet when you spend time with them, a very different picture emerges. One or both individuals may be indifferent, cold, disdainful or even nasty and cruel in the way they talk to and act toward their mate. What is even more astonishing is that these individuals may stay together for many years, or until one dies. Why do they remain together? Poor self-images (how you feel about yourself, and what you feel you deserve in relationships and in life in general) are often at the root of this seemingly bizarre behavior.

<> <> <>

In a good relationship, if you ask each individual how the other shows their caring for them, each person can readily rattle off a number of loving behaviors. This in not the case in troubled relationships.

Some people ask whether it is better to surprise their mate at the last minute with vacation plans or to tell them sometime in advance. While both approaches have their advantages and disadvantages, by telling your mate in advance enables them to enjoy the *anticipation* of a great vacation, which is days, weeks, or even months away. This can make the period of time *leading* up to the actual trip more enjoyable for the individual as well as having the pleasure of experiencing the actual vacation.

<> <> <>

In a loving relationship, when a physical and/or psychological trauma occurs to one of the individuals, the couple gets emotionally closer, and focuses their energies on how best to deal with the problem or problems. In contrast, in a troubled relationship, the individual not directly having the problem may feel "put upon" by their partners' problem or problems leading to friction between them, and a distancing may occur, culminating in the end of the relationship in some instances.

<> <> <>

As a couple grows closer over the years, typically much can be communicated to one another without actually saying a word.

If a couple is arguing over an issue that does not seem to be reaching any constructive resolution, then ask each other if this is of major or of minor importance to each person. If they both state that it is actually of minor importance, then a good hug, and "Let's let it go" can be a good mutual solution.

<> <> <>

It is a wonderful experience to meet people who dramatically impact in a positive way on other people's lives.

<> <> <>

Many young people go for schooling for years in pursuit of careers largely based on their *fantasies* of how it will be to work in a given profession. It would be beneficial for these young people to volunteer at these jobs in order to get a *realistic* flavor of what these jobs entail. This would help prevent a number of them from wasting years of training in pursuit of a career that they do not enjoy or perhaps even intensely dislike.

It is amazing how many individuals tell one or both of their parents the most intimate details of their lives, including their marriages, even in their 20's, 30's, and even older. It is interesting that these parents tend to be extremely judgmental and especially critical. It is important that such individuals significantly limit what they share from their personal lives with these parents as it is disrespectful to yourself and your spouse to share intimate aspects of your life and especially your marriage with others, particularly insensitive parents.

<> <> <>

Sometimes, couples will tell their own parents about problems that they are having with their spouse. This is generally unwise and can change the relationship between the in-laws and their son or daughter-in-law. Even if the couple works out their problems and make up, their parents are still "stuck" with their angry and/or hurtful feelings toward their adult child's mate.

<> <> <>

Psychologically immature individuals pick their careers almost entirely based on *salary* and *prestige*. Psychologically mature people, while they certainly consider these two factors, primarily make their decision on the basis of *quality of their lives*.

Some parents, upon hearing from their adult child how badly their spouse is treating them will "take on" the allegedly offensive partner. Instead of the couple trying to resolve their differences with or without professional help, this parent keeps arguing with their son-in-law or daughter-in-law. This is extremely destructive to the marriage and infantalizing on the part of the aggressive parent in their attempt to "help" their adult child.

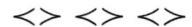

<> <> <>

It is important to learn when your mate needs time alone. These are instances when being alone for a short time is the perfect behavior to help your partner work out a troublesome issue or simply mellow out. Knowing when to do this can be much appreciated.

<> <> <>

There are a few clients who believe that since they are paying for the psychologist's services, that they "own" their psychotherapy time, as well as the psychologist. These attitudes and their ramifications need to be explored at the beginning of the therapy.

<> <> <>

In a dysfunctional family, an individual may end up having one or more friends who are more caring to them than *any* of their family members. If this individual feels closer to these friends than to their family, then this is *perfectly* understandable under the circumstances.

If you met each of your family members at a party, and they were each strangers to you, what would you think of each of them? Would you ever want to develop a friendship with any of them? Why or why not?

<> <> <>

When you were growing up, who could you open your heart to in your family? Would they try to listen to you and comfort you in a loving, respectful and sensitive manner?

<> <> <>

In some dysfunctional families, there are sometimes "generals" and "foot soldiers." The "generals" periodically do selfish, self-centered and even cruel things to one or more family members while other family members, the "foot soldiers," support and defend any and all hurtful, mean, and selfish behavior of the "generals." Ultimately, in this situation, it may be best for the victims of this abuse to *permanently* separate from these cruel family members.

<> <> <>

Some individuals do not respect other people's *boundaries*. They see nothing wrong with violating another person's rights or feelings in order to get their needs met. They love to tell others how to live their lives. However, they do *not* like it at all if others try to tell *them* what to do. It is important to either set firm limits with these controlling, overbearing individuals, or, if this cannot be done, to seriously consider ending the relationship.

Some individuals believe that once an argument has quieted down that all is forgiven. In fact, one sex (generally men) sometimes think that this is the "perfect" time to relate sexually. In fact, the vast majority of the time, this is a big mistake as strong feelings often take some *time* to change.

<> <> <>

Some people become successful in their business ventures by exhibiting such traits as being extremely aggressive. These people need to learn that while these behavior may have contributed significantly to their successful careers, this is *not* the way to relate to your family and to your friends. It is sad how many individuals have never learned this discrimination.

<> <> <>

Some people have had such psychologically painful experiences that they appear to have become emotionally "frozen" at the moment that this trauma occurred. They need to go for psychotherapy if they are going to be able to work out this trauma or traumas in their lives in order to go *forward* with their lives both emotionally and socially.

Our society needs to value and recognize as many *different* areas of constructive achievement by its citizens as is reasonably possible. There are many, many talented people in our society whose gifts and achievements are not properly valued by our society, and thus contribute to these people having a low self-image.

<> <> <>

Some people take themselves much too seriously. It is a sweet and endearing quality to occasionally poke gentle fun at oneself.

<> <> <>

Our society largely wastes the talents of our elderly, retired individuals. A number of these people have great skills that are not being utilized to help assist, train, and educate others. We need to actively enlist their help in making our society, and the people in it function at a significantly higher level. These elderly, retired individuals would feel more productive and better about themselves as they contribute to improving the quality of the lives of their fellow citizens.

<> <> <>

Psychologically healthy people are *realistic* in discriminating what they can change in their lives and what they cannot.

Some individuals do not seem to "shape up" in a relationship until their partner appears to be at "their wit's end" and ready to end the relationship. If this becomes a pattern, the partner should indeed say "goodbye." Their partner obviously knows how to "behave properly" but chooses *not* to until they *have* to.

<> <> <>

If an individual generally acts in a respectful, friendly manner with other people, but is very selfish and inconsiderate when relating to their spouse, then the latter should seriously consider terminating the relationship. This is because this person obviously does know how to behave appropriately when they choose to do so, but does not want to do so with their mate.

<> <> <>

Some people, when they are arguing with their spouse, are quick to talk about a divorce. Unless these people are sincere about doing this, they should not try to "emotionally blackmail" their partner during an argument. It is cruel and destructive behavior.

Dinner time can be wonderful as a family bonding experience. People often relax while enjoying good food. As a result, some enjoyable family conversation can occur. It is sad that some families have a policy of *not* talking to one another while at the dinner table. It is also sad that fewer and fewer families make time to eat together.

<> <> <>

If an individual gives a "little extra" of themselves it can sometimes generate considerable benefits. For example, if the boss asks you to start your work day at 8:00 a.m., and you consistently arrive at 7:30 a.m., this minor extra giving of yourself can help distinguish yourself from your co-workers. If you study the careers of very successful people, a number of them have gone the "extra mile" in their road to success. Try doing it!

<> <> <>

Some people are both extremely kind-hearted as well as being very competent. As a result, they tend to attract overly dependent and parasitic individuals who want these individuals to do things *for them*. It is important that these good-hearted, competent people *protect themselves* by sometimes saying "No" to other people's requests and demands in order to protect themselves physically and emotionally from "burning out."

It is a *major* accomplishment for a couple to achieve what I like to call a "mutual loving trust." This means that each member of the relationship *truly* believes that the other person always has good intentions toward them, and therefore, they are *never* trying to be malicious or purposefully hurtful toward them. Couples who achieve this "mutual loving trust" will almost never have ugly fights or arguments as a result.

<> <> <>

There are some individuals who appear to have lost touch with the soft, gentle, tender parts of their personalities. They almost always present themselves as being "hard," tough, angry and ready to do battle. Psychologically mature people tend to shy away from relating to these individuals as they appear to have lost touch with their "humanity," namely the *best* parts of being a human being.

<> <> <>

We tend to be a very *judgmental* and *critical* society. This tends to create individuals who have poor self-images (how they feel about themselves), and poor relating skills.

It is amazing that all our citizens are not anxious and very depressed, as well as being extremely fearful. This is because our news media appears preoccupied with reporting all kinds of horrendous events happening in all parts of the world. Whether it is a devastating natural catastrophe occurring somewhere in the world, or the murder or sexual molestation of an individual, or perhaps the ominous possibility of developing cancer or heart disease, our media seems to be determined to present their "misery news." How about presenting a *more balanced* portrayal of what is happening locally, nationally and internationally, with at least as many happy, constructive, positive events or human interactions being cited as well as the most traumatic? This would help people to have some positive environmental information for their psyches and intellects to digest which would help them emotionally and attitudinally.

<> <> <>

What helps a loving relationship to endure? One crucial area deals with how our mate treats *other* people in their daily lives. How does your spouse treat the grocer, the gas station attendant, the waiter at a restaurant or their mailman? Your mate may treat you well, but if they do *not* treat these other individuals with kindness and respect, then over time, this can cause you to lose respect and caring for your mate. Many professionals and lay people fail to recognize the importance of this variable when they try to understand why one relationship is prospering while another is withering away.

What is a particularly nice compliment that someone could genuinely pay you that would truly touch your heart? Why is this so?

<> <> <>

What is a talent or hobby that you would really like to cultivate? What is stopping you from doing this?

<> <> <>

What are some of the wisest words that have been spoken to you?
What are some of the best words of advice that you ever gave to another person?

<> <> <>

Listen to the way that other people laugh. It will tell you something about their personality. For example, psychologically healthy individuals tend to laugh heartily, their entire body involved. In essence, they laugh just like an infant or little children laugh. In contrast, some individuals laugh in an uptight constricted manner, as if they were trying to control how they laugh. Still other people laugh in an outrageously loud manner, and you can sense their underlying anger and hostility in this kind of laugh. How do you laugh?

Some couples are *forever* changing things. They are forever moving from one house to the other, or they are constantly buying new wardrobes. They may be constantly changing their jobs, and changing friends. What these couples *really* want to change in many instances, is to change their partners or spouses.

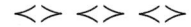

<> <> <>

Some people are constantly having plastic surgery on various parts of their bodies. When asked why they are doing this, they often state that they do not like the way they look, and they therefore want to look better. In reality, in a number of instances, these individuals' problems actually revolve around having a poor or low self-image. As a result, they do *not* need plastic surgery. What they *do* need is psychotherapy.

<> <> <>

It is interesting that some married couples have such problems relating to each other, but are *so* much better parents. These individuals tend to treat their children in a warm, loving, respectful manner, and in general, have loving, caring relationships with them. This indicates that these individuals do have the capabilities to be loving and respectful, but for some reason or reasons they are not doing so with their spouses. This observation needs to be explored in psychotherapy.

If you want to get a rough idea of how self-centered a person is, listen to the pronouns that they use when they are speaking. Overly self-centered, selfish peoples' speech is filled with "I" and "me" statements as opposed to frequent use of "you," "us" and "we" statements. These individuals' behavior will tend to corroborate these words.

<> <> <>

People who have experienced psychologically and/or materially difficult early years, may forever be striving for and are satisfied when things are nice and peaceful. These people are perfectly happy with going on vacation to the same place year after year or ordering the same meal at the same restaurant every time they dine out. In contrast, people who have experienced happier early lives, want *more* than this. They want *new* and exciting experiences as much as possible. This can lead to conflicts between these different personalities.

<> <> <>

Some individuals are forever complaining that it bothers them that they have to make some changes in order to have a good relationship with their mate. In discussing this with these people, they often state that they want to be *themselves*. For many of these individuals this means just acting anyway they want to act, and saying whatever is on their mind. These same individuals seem ideally suited for living by *themselves*. In fact, depending on the degree to which they desire to be themselves and do their "own thing," perhaps they would do best being hermits, and thus they would not have to consider anyone elses' rights or feelings.

When you are about to have a difficult, emotionally charged conversation with another person, try to decide in advance what your goals are in having this talk. If possible, explain these goals at the outset of your conversation, and ask the other person what their goals are. This procedure can help to make each individual more receptive to listening to the other, and to keep the conversation focused.

<> <> <>

It is wise to spend time with elderly people. You can learn a great deal about how you want to live your life if you are fortunate enough to reach an advanced age in reasonably good physical health. Some things you will want to emulate, and some you will plan to do very differently. In general, it is being wise and constructive to have a number of good older role models as we go through our lives.

<> <> <>

Some people appear to *relish* and put large amounts of energy in defying authority figures. Whether it involves not doing assigned homework; not following the directions of a supervisor at work; or not taking prescription drugs as directed by your doctor, these individuals appear to be determined to *defy* these authority figures. In many cases, they may cause themselves unneeded problems and difficulties seemingly unconcerned about the consequences of their actions. This defiant orientation can actually ruin their lives as well as that of loved ones who depend on these same people.

Sometimes during particularly trying times, people are amazed and gratified at how well they are able to cope under the most trying circumstances. This "rising to the occasion" by these individuals can be among the proudest moments of their lives.

<> <> <>

Some of the most competent and responsible people desperately could use on a course entitled, "How to Have Fun." In their drive to get ahead, they have apparently lost touch with the capacity to *enjoy* themselves. They need to regain this capacity if they are to experience a truly enriching life. They should start such a course immediately.

<> <> <>

If you ask someone for an opinion about something, you do not have the right to judge their response, or try to control what they say. Remember, *you* asked them for *their* opinion. Allow them to respond freely.

<> <> <>

Some people are forever *gossiping* about other individuals. They love to put everybody around down, uttering one criticism after the other. These people tend to be very unhappy, and they appear to lead miserable, empty lives. They should be focusing on improving the quality of their *own* lives, rather than wasting energy in trashing other people.

There are some individuals who love to champion all kinds of admirable causes. Yet, in their every day dealing with individual people, they tend to be rude, inconsiderate, selfish and self-centered. These people really do not appear to care about the individuals affected by their causes. Instead, they are driven by their *own* narcissistic needs and desires.

<> <> <>

Some husbands and fathers are forever doing projects around the house. While this may initially be viewed by their family as being helpful, if this occurs too frequently then the same family members may become disgruntled and disenchanted with these projects. In these instances, the husband and father may be using these household projects as a manipulation so as *not* to relate to the other family members. This behavior needs to be addressed and worked out to the satisfaction of all family members involved.

<> <> <>

Some individuals who are the sole financial support for their family, sometimes use this position to "bully" the other members of their family. They may use their position as the sole wage owner to insist that they have the final say in all major family matters. They may also periodically refer to the other members of the family as being "parasites." This state of affairs has to be dealt with swiftly, even if the marriage has to be dissolved. Also, it is a major reason that more and more women are raising their daughters to get a good education, and get a good job so as not to be at the mercy of "bullying" husbands or boyfriends.

Look in the mirror. What do you see? Would you like to be this person? Why or why not?

<> <> <>

One way of communicating to your child that you respect them, is to periodically ask their opinion on various issues. This does *not* mean that you have to agree with every one of their opinions, or that you have to *act* on each of them. Rather, you are communicating that you value hearing what they are thinking and what they have today. Some parents almost never treat their children with this show of respect.

<> <> <>

In general, the psychologically healthier a person is, the more realistic body image they possess. In contrast, some individuals (i.e., anorexia nervosa's) can look in the mirror with their ribs protruding, and state that they are "too fat" (and they mean it).

Many families in our country make birthdays and anniversaries a very special time. These occasions are among the happiest days experienced during the year. However, there are families that do not even give each other gifts during these occasions. These families do not make "a big deal" out of these times. In a relationship, if one member comes from the former type of family, and the other from the latter type, it is important that the individual from the family that does not really make a big deal of birthdays, still show caring and respect for their partner by making these days special for their mate. Not doing so, can cause marked hurt feelings in their partner, and cause a rift in the relationship.

<> <> <>

In some relationships, one of the members may continuously be very difficult for the other member to deal with. Almost every request by the latter is met by some resistance, negativism, and even outright defiance. The belabored partner may even lament that if they would make a request or suggestion, and their mate said "fine," that they would "faint." This is the kind of partner that an individual would do well to terminate the relationship with. Peacefulness is certainly preferable to continuous aggravation.

<> <> <>

Nature provides us continually with *many* beautiful and wondrous spectacles. Find someone to share these awesome gifts with.

Three major reasons why relationships fail are in-laws, money, and sex. Couples that are in agreement, and work as a team with respect to these three areas have a significantly better chance of having a happy and successful relationship.

<> <> <>

It is a wise thing to periodically map out what one's goals are in life, and how successful we are being in reaching these goals at the present time. We should also ask ourselves if we are not making good progress in reaching one or more of our goals, "What do I need to do differently to be more efficient in achieving what I want to achieve?"

<> <> <>

Psychologically mature people are very good at "picking their battles." In essence, they are aware that they cannot argue with their partner about every little inconvenience or difference of opinion. When these people do take a stand, it is for a very good reason, and they express themselves in a firm, yet respectful, easily receptive manner.

The morning is a particularly fertile time for major family arguments to arise. The various family members are typically rushing to meet time deadlines, and as such, are usually tense and irritable. It is a wise maneuver for each family to sit down one evening the beginning of each month, and discuss how the morning hustle and bustle in the house is progressing. If conducted in an empathetic and constructive manner, these monthly meetings can help prevent many potential family altercations. Try it!

<> <> <>

In several instances, I have heard individuals complain that they are about to make a major change in their careers, and their mate is not equally enthusiastic, and may not even approve of these future changes. Actually, it is very easy to be supportive of your partner's plans if you agree with them. However, it is significantly *more loving* when you do not really agree with your mate's career change, but out of love and respect for your partner, you still will be supportive and encouraging. This is an *especially loving* behavior.

<> <> <>

It is very nice to relate to another individual whose words, actions and tones all coincide. Many of us get confused when relating to other people, because these three parameters do not convey the same message.

If you have to cancel a date with another person, and you want to demonstrate your disappointment as well as your genuine desire to get together in the near future, simply say the following: "Let's get out our calendars right now, and make a definite date to get together soon. When is your next available date? My next opening is. . . ." This is a nice way to rectify the present situation. Try it!

<> <> <>

If you are the kind of person who tends to get down and even "clobber" yourself when things go wrong, it is very important not to get involved with "blamers," namely people who immediately blame others when things are going their way. These "blamers" will prove to be particularly toxic to your self-image.

<> <> <>

It is important for parents to try to expose their children to as many positive and interesting experiences as possible. This will help make them more receptive to all the special things that life has to offer them as they go through their lives.

All couples sometimes feel that they are in a "rut." One helpful suggestion is for such a couple to sit down, and decide on an activity that they both can do on a regular basis together. For example, they may decide to sign up for weekly ballroom dancing lessons, or join the gym and try to go perhaps three times or so each week. This will set aside couples time for them as they engage in a new activity *together*. Make sure that you pick an activity you *both* will enjoy.

<> <> <>

I once had an evening psychology student tell me that her husband was complaining that her going to evening college classes was "ruining our sex lives." This was an unwise and unloving selfish statement on the part of her spouse. Actually, if he supported his wife's desire to take a couple of evening college classes, she would probably feel happier and more fulfilled. Support and encouragement over this endeavor by her husband might well lead to *more* frequent and better quality sex.

<> <> <>

It is a sad commentary that so many school systems are now making kindergarten an academically oriented year for our children. As in the past, kindergarten should be a *fun* and *playful* time.

Some people feel they were never given the proper parenting that they deserved as a child. They forever are viewing other people consciously or unconsciously as potential parents who will make up for the deprivation and possibly abuse they experienced during their childhood with respect to parenting. They may even go so far as to call other people, "mother" or "mommy." Also, their expectations of these people are totally unreasonable as they are *not* their parents. If someone tries to put you in this position, it is important for your own emotional well-being to correct them and state accurately, for example, that "I am your friend not your mother (or father)."

<> <> <>

It is important that parents teach their children as they grow up to think for themselves. Although it is important in life to be able to get along with, and in general, follow the requests of authority figures, it is also very important to use your own judgment when potential emergencies arise. Listening to your inner self in these dire circumstances have helped even save people's lives, while blindly following an authority figures commands could have resulted in one's death.

<> <> <>

Sometimes, genuinely stating that, "I made a mistake. I take full responsibility for what happened as a result, and I plan to correct the problem as soon as possible," may nip a problem in the bud.

Each household has its own feeling tone or emotional ambiance. For example, some households have serene, warm emotional tones; some have an anxious and depressed emotional tone, while still others have an angry, hostile emotional tone. What kind of emotional tone permeates your family? Do you personally, radiate the same or a different emotional tone?

<> <> <>

Ask your child what they like best about you. Also, ask them what they would like you to change, and why. This information could be very helpful for you to learn as a parent.

<> <> <>

Ask your child what qualities they think you like best about them. Also, ask them if there are any qualities or behaviors of theirs, that you would like them to change. This information could prove to be very educational.

<> <> <>

There are special moments of quiet happiness, when as parents you are out socially with your adult children, and they appear to be happy and well in their life pursuits.

There appear to be moments when we become physically ill, so that our bodies are forcing us to stop and take some time to reflect on the current status of how we are living our lives, and to assess whether any changes are in order. Realization of this opportunity for reflection, and self-evaluation can lead to some very helpful insights and proactive behaviors.

<> <> <>

There are certain activities that when people engage in them they forget how old they actually are, and once again, feel that they are at a significantly younger age. Aerobic exercising at the gym, dancing and outdoor activities such as skiing can sometimes cause people to feel significantly younger, as they lose themselves in these type of activities. This can be an exhilarating experience.

<> <> <>

The majority of couples who come for psychotherapy have a goal of trying to improve their relationship. However, there are individuals as well as couples who have other agendas that they are trying to follow by coming for treatment. It is important for the psychologist to confront this individual or couple with respect to this underlying motivation or motivations if anything is going to be accomplished.

Some individuals are indeed their own worst enemies. These people appear to be experts at creating additional stresses for themselves as they go through their lives. They wait until the very last minute to study for examinations, or they begin a paper the night before it is due. They go running around paying their bills at the last minute, when they could have paid them much sooner. Instead of making life easier for themselves they seem to make it much more difficult than it has to be. They need to examine in psychotherapy why they have such a need to burden themselves in order to live a happier, more stress-free life.

<> <> <>

If you find yourself humming or even singing a song without initially being aware of doing so, pay attention to the content of the song as well as the mood being conveyed by it. This may provide you with some valuable insight as to your present emotional state as well as any present daily concern.

<> <> <>

Some individuals cannot seem to tolerate when relationships are too peaceful. They have a need to start conflicts between themselves and family members and friends. This seems to make them feel more secure, even though it can cause emotional upheaval with others. These kind of people you would do well to try to avoid.

There are some individuals who love to argue with others. They find it stimulating, exciting and in some cases, even sexually arousing. These basically are unstable individuals who can be extremely toxic to other people. Try to stay away from them.

<> <> <>

There are some individuals who need to be the center of attention at all times. They will go out of their way to gain this position at all costs. They are the individuals who may suddenly become ill at a wedding, in order to take some of the attention from the bride and groom, and to gain some of it for themselves. Knowing this about these individuals can be very helpful in coping with their behavior.

<> <> <>

Psychiatric drugs can be very helpful in helping individuals cope with emotional and behavioral problems in some instances. While the media seems to enjoy portraying these drugs as being horrible, this is blatantly untrue. If these drugs are prescribed properly, and the patients use them as directed, then they can help many people have unpleasant symptoms mitigated and in some cases, even eliminated so that these people can feel and cope significantly better.

Some individuals who have been in psychotherapy like to play amateur psychologist. They love to tell friends and relatives about their personal and interpersonal deficiencies, and how "out of touch" these people are with their true selves. What these people are actually demonstrating by these destructive behavior, is that their own therapy experience was far from successfully completed.

<> <> <>

Some parents are obsessed with their children learning and obeying a multitude of rigid rules that they have created for them. Over time, their children learn that these rules are more important to these parents than are their childrens' feeling or needs. This can be extremely hurtful and damaging to these children.

<> <> <>

It would be of great benefit to your marriage, if you genuinely make an appreciative comment to your spouse, even occasionally. For example, if your spouse has been working particularly hard and coming home at a late hour as a result, it would typically warm your mate's heart if you acknowledge their efforts by saying, "I really appreciate how hard you have been working for me and our family. Thank you so much." Similarly, if your mate has been staying up late at night to have your dinner waiting for you when you come home at a very late hour, it would typically be much appreciated if you said, "I feel so good when I come home, and you are waiting up for me with a great dinner. Thank you so much." These comments are what helps keep marriages alive and well.

It is an absolutely wonderful feeling to know that someone you deeply love, also loves you with all their heart.

<> <> <>

It is a wonderful feeling if you ask someone for some needed help, and they respond by genuinely saying, "Thank you for giving me the opportunity to help you. I'll do whatever I can to be of help."

<> <> <>

Some people believe that if you are upset or angry with another person, or they feel this way about you that the result has to be an ugly confrontation. In reality, this does *not* have to be the case at all. If both individuals take turns in clearly expressing how they feel about what has been transpiring, and the other person listens quietly, and is given the same courtesy when they talk about their own feelings and thoughts about the situation, then they have a good chance to work out the situation in a constructive manner.

<> <> <>

Who were your favorite teachers in school? What made them special to you?

In some relationships, one or both individuals almost always immediately side with the *other* party when their mate discusses a problem that they are having with this person. Even when their mate appears to have been obviously wronged by the other person, their spouse refuses to take their side. This may occur because the spouses' parents almost always took the other persons' side when *they* were growing up. This kind of behavior can damage the bond between this couple if it is not worked out.

<> <> <>

When appropriate, using numbers (i.e., scales or percentages) can be very helpful to the psychologist in understanding their clients' feelings better. For example, two clients may both report that they are feeling better since they started coming for psychotherapy sessions. When asked by the psychologist what percent they mean, I have heard clients use these same words to mean from 10% to perhaps 80%. This gives the psychologist a better "feel" for what their clients' words actually mean.

<> <> <>

The transition from high school to college is typically extremely stressful. For example, our friends' daughter who had been calling her mother, "mom" since she was three years old, suddenly started calling her "mommy" her entire freshman year at her boarding college. Once she returned home during the following summer, she once again started to call her mother, "mom." When her mother pointed out this behavior to her, she was absolutely amazed.

Some individuals suffer from "time urgency." They are constantly preoccupied with not being late, and actually are very *early* the vast majority of the time. Unfortunately, these "tightly wound" people tend to *impose* this intolerance on to others.

<> <> <>

It is important to pay attention to cues coming from within our body. For example, if you are in a situation, and begin to feel very fearful, *listen* to your feelings and try to remove yourself from this situation. In some cases, people have reported having saved their life by listening to these intense feelings and responding to them.

<> <> <>

In a good relationship, there is an increasing appreciation of your mate, and their efforts to keep the relationship alive and well. There also is an indescribable warmth and tenderness that grows over time. The "magic" between the two of you glows as brightly as ever.

Some teachers and school systems give great amounts of homework to their students. They proudly proclaim that this contributes to showing what a great education these students are receiving. In fact, an overabundance of such homework, may, in fact, "burn out" their students and help contribute to developing a poor attitude toward school and learning in general.

<> <> <>

The best parents *respect* as well as love their children. This is demonstrated in their words and actions toward them.

<> <> <>

It is a wonderful experience to be in a profession where you can touch many people in a positive way so as to make the rest of their lives happier and more fulfilling.

It is important that psychologists and other professionals that do psychotherapy periodically take breaks from their practice if they are to remain fresh and effective in helping their clients and patients. It is the responsibility of every professional working in this area to guard against "burn out" from occurring.

<> <> <>

Looking back, did you ever notice that for an entire day you were a bit overly tense, sensitive and irritable and you had no idea why you were feeling this way? One possibility is that you had an *upsetting dream* the night before that you did not recall. Realizing this possibility can be helpful in some instances.

<> <> <>

Many people dream about loved ones being hurt or even killed in accidents and the like. They often cry out while they are having such dreams and even scream out loud. One of the most common reasons for such a dream is that we are *angry* at this loved one.

It is important for parents to set aside at least a few minutes each day to ask their child how their day was. This helps create a daily dialogue between the parent and their child, which hopefully will carry over into the childs' future marriage if this occurs. This "keeping in touch" will help keep the parent and their child and subsequent marital partner on the right track for the relationships to be alive and well.

<> <> <>

A number of parents whose children are in kindergarten are being told that there appears to be a problem since there child is not yet reading. Some of these parents are being advised to have their child evaluated professionally to see why this is. This appears to be very unreasonable as past generations of our children were not expected to learn to read until they were in the first grade. This practice needs to be discontinued as it is causing numerous parents and their children unwarranted anxiety.

<> <> <>

If you are the parents of more than one child, it is important for each parent to spend *individual* time with each of these children. This will help forge a good emotional bond between each parent and each one of their children. Some families only seem to spend the vast majority of their time together in a group, and while this is also important, the child and the parent will benefit from this individual attention.

Some individuals are forever spending considerable money on new clothes and new cars. They are forever going to the "best" restaurants. In some cases, they are behaving in this manner in order to feel better about themselves. Their *real* problem revolves around a low self-image, and the harboring of a lot of painful feelings. In essence, they need to look *inside* of themselves instead of outside. These individuals require psychotherapy, *not* more material things.

<> <> <>

It is interesting and revealing that some individuals who ordinarily almost never ask their spouse their opinion, suddenly have to consult them when the child asks them for something. The "asking spouse" is being cowardly and manipulative. Instead of telling the child directly that they will not be able to assist you, they now put the onus on their mate in an endeavor to make them appear to be the "bad one." It would not be surprising if these same individuals when they disagree with a desire of their children instead state, "I'll have to talk this over with your father (mother)." They are using this tactic to once again be the "good one," and the spouse appearing to again be the "bad one." This represents extremely unloving behavior.

<> <> <>

It is a wonderful feeling when as a parent you genuinely compliment your child, and you see their *whole face light up.*

It is very emotionally beneficial to spend a few minutes sitting on the side of your childs' bed when they are about to go to sleep. Some of the gentlest and sweetest talks can sometimes occur during these times. It is a wonderful thing for both the parent and the child to end the childs' day on such a loving note. Try it!

<> <> <>

Some couples who enter psychotherapy are looking for the psychologist to judge or even blame the other person. In actuality, the function of the psychologist is neither. The psychologist is there to *help*; not to judge or blame anyone.

<> <> <>

When faced with a number of tasks, it is important to prioritize the importance of each. By dealing with the most important tasks first, the individual can be maximally effective in using their time well. This will help reduce stress.

Some individuals appear to "fall to pieces" when a problem arises in their lives. These individuals need to construct a mental stress scale ranging from 10 (life or death situations) down to 1 (of minimal significance). By placing the present adverse situation in its appropriate place on this scale (i.e., "3"), this may help the individual put this problem in perspective, and enhance their ability to solve it.

<> <> <>

From the moment a baby is born, they are constantly *interacting* with their mother. If the baby regularly smiles, coos and giggles during these interactions, the mother will tend to be encouraged to relate more lovingly to her infant. If, on the other hand, the infant tends to cry, whine and be irritable in the mother's presence, over time, she will tend to become less loving and warm to her baby. However, many personality theorists as well as numerous psychiatrists and psychologists continue to *ignore* this interaction, instead continuing to *blame* the mother in a vacuum for causing her infant to later develop emotional and social problems.

<> <> <>

Some personality theorists and practicing professionals believe that our personalities are *totally* shaped by our life experiences (our environment). Others believe that our personalities are totally genetically determined and are "set in stone" at birth. In my opinion , we are born with a definite, genetically based personality which will be "fine tuned" by our environment over our lifespan.

When a person is truly "shocked" when their spouse wants to end their relationship, this is a sad commentary on how "tuned in" they were to each other, and specifically to each others *needs*.

<> <> <>

If you want to be maximally effective in dealing with representatives of department stores or credit card companies, it is important to clearly differentiate for these individuals that you are angry or disgruntled with some *policy* being practiced by the company, and *not at all* with this person who is merely trying to help you. Implementing this technique from the beginning of the conversation can significantly enhance your chances of getting your needs met by this company representative since if the latter thinks that you are angry with *them* as well, they will tend to become defensive and antagonistic. Try this technique.

<> <> <>

Having worked with many couples in psychotherapy over the years, I can state unequivocally, that the number one reason a relationship ultimately ends is *selfishness* on the part of one or both parties.

It is amusing, but yet sad, that so many middle aged and senior males believe that they "deserve" young, attractive women as companions. They feel that dating women of their own chronological age is settling for "second best." These men need only to look in the mirror after taking a shower, and more importantly to look inside of themselves to see the errors in their ways.

<> <> <>

There are a number of individuals who totally rely on their own intellects and rationality to guide how they behave. If you tell this type of individual that they are behaving in a hurtful manner toward you, or that you are frightened about something, they will often appear perplexed, commenting, "In my mind, you are being irrational." In essence, in these instances your feelings or your fears are not considered important at all. They truly believe that "You just have to become rational," namely agreeing with *their* rational perspective. In actuality, these "rational people" are extremely selfish and self-centered. They are very controlling. They do *not* understand that if you care about another person, their feelings and fears should be valued and addressed, not judged and invariably criticized. These "rational" individuals may be destined to spend many a cold winter night alone with their "rational minds."

<> <> <>

It is interesting to note that some of the wealthier people in your social circle may also be the most insecure and worried about their finances.

It is unfortunate, but there are a significant number of individuals who put money in front of their family in terms of their priorities. Such individuals will pay a *price* both overtly and covertly for this selfishness.

<> <> <>

Some adult children are forever talking about the money that they will inherit from their parents when the latter pass away. This is a very selfish, self-centered and unloving way to behave.

<> <> <>

The longer one studies the field of interpersonal relationships, the more you become aware that there is always so much *more* that can be learned.

<> <> <>

Some people state that they would *never* go for psychotherapy for themselves as everyone has their "problems." This is a naive and overly simplistic point of view. The range of human psychological and behavioral problems range from mild all the way to severe with all the intermediate levels. As such, we may all have psychological and behavioral problems, but the range is *huge*. Also, why would an individual not want to have the *best quality of life* that they can attain?

Human beings tend to like to have "closure" with respect to emotionally charged issues. They will even sometimes adapt unrealistic or irrational viewpoints in order to feel better and bring this "closure" concerning an individual or a situation that is troubling them. For example, when a person feels that another individual has "wronged them," they may "stew" about this for days or much longer until they confidently conclude that, "What goes around, comes around!" or "He/she will get theirs!" Even though this may *never actually* occur, the individual believing this, often will state that they now feel "much better."

<> <> <>

There are some individuals who are forever worrying that they have offended their sweetheart or a friend. They are constantly inquiring if they have offended the other person, even when there is no reason for them to be thinking this way. One good way to help this person deal with this problem is to state, "I promise you that if anything is truly bothering me, that I will absolutely tell you, and we will work it out. If I don't mention anything then you can be sure that everything is fine with us as far as I am concerned." This technique has helped a number of relationships when this problem has arisen.

There are some extremely toxic individuals who are constantly trying to "brainwash" their mate. They attempt to do this by constantly telling the other person that whatever they are thinking and feeling is incorrect, and their perceptions are all distorted. In essence, these highly toxic individuals are trying to convince their mate that they cannot trust *themselves*, and instead, must rely on the other person to tell them how to think, feel, perceive, and even behave properly, according to the toxic individual. This person is bad for ones' psychological health, and needs to be gotten rid of immediately.

<> <> <>

What are five of your major goals in life? How are you going about trying to attain them?

<> <> <>

Every individual should be fortunate enough to have had at least one teacher in school who stimulated their minds and touched their hearts. Specifically, such a teacher really will excite and stimulate their students as to the joy and privilege it is to be exposed to and to learn this area of knowledge, and through this growth process to become a better person in their own way. These teachers will be giving their students one of the great gifts of being a member of this society. These special teachers should be forever remembered, and cherished by those students who were lucky enough to be associated with and taught by them. Have you been fortunate enough to have such a teacher? What grade did you have them, and what subject did they teach?

There will come a day when people in our society no longer talk about their retirement. So many people have equated retiring from their jobs with in essence, withdrawing from life and passively waiting to die. Instead, more modern individuals will speak about going on to a new chapter or phase of their lives. Given good health, good financial resources, and a good companion, this next period could be the *best* period of an individuals' whole life!

<> <> <>

If you met someone at a social gathering who was exactly like you, what would you think of them? What would you like about this person? Is there anything you would dislike?

<> <> <>

While there are many parents who are very concerned about how their children are being treated by their teachers in the classroom, there also needs to be attention paid to how their children are being treated by their coaches in the various sports offered in schools, particularly at the high school level. Specifically, I have observed coaches who have been given glowing reviews in the local newspapers who in actuality have gotten in their players faces as they proceeded to verbally abuse them. I have heard them talk as if a given game represented "life or death" for the various players. In essence, there needs to be much closer monitoring of these coaches and the abusive ones reprimanded and even removed, irrespective of whether they have an impressive winning record.

If you could spend an evening with any famous person, living or dead, who would you pick? Why would you select them? What would your evening consist of?

<> <> <>

In this era of narcissism and entitlement, it is becoming increasingly rare to find individuals who "keep their word." While it does not take great intelligence, a wonderful personality or great looks to behave in such a manner, it is very gratifying to have such a person in your life. Value and enjoy them.